A·C·T·I·O·N B·O·O·K

FLY THE SPACE SHUTTLE

Carole Stott

DK PUBLISHING, INC.

A DK PUBLISHING BOOK

Project Editor Claire Bampton
Editor Francesca Stich
Senior Editor Sue Leonard
US Editor Camela Decaire
Art Editors Jane Bull, Cathy Chesson, Vicky Wharton
Picture Researcher Monica Allende
Photographers Andy Crawford, Gary Ombler
Paper Engineer David Hawcock

Illustrator Hans Jenssen

Managing Editor Sarah Phillips
Senior Managing Art Editor Peter Bailey
DTP Designers Karen Nettelfield, Andrew O'Brien
Design Assistant Miranda May
Production Joanne Blackmore, Lauren Britton

First American Edition, 1997

2 4 6 8 10 9 7 5 3 1

Published in the United States by
DK Publishing, Inc.
95 Madison Avenue,
New York, New York 10016

Visit us on the World Wide Web at http://www.dk.com

Copyright © 1997 Dorling Kindersley Limited, London

Published in Great Britain by Dorling Kindersley Limited.

A catalog record is available from the Library of Congress.

ISBN: 0-7894-2021-X

Color reproduction by Flying Colours, Italy.
Manufactured in China for Imago.

Identification badge

There are hundreds of people
working at the Space Center.
Everyone wears a badge so you
know instantly who they are and
what their role is. Here is your
badge. Please add your details
and photograph to it now, so
that your training can begin.

In the Space
Center you should
display your badge
at all times.

Space Center

Glue a
photograph of
yourself in here.

Name ....

Age ....

Height ....

Signature ....

Training Tasks

Your training is divided into
four modules, each made up
a number of training sessions
Each module is taught by an
instructor who will assign a
training task at the end of the
session. Work through the
training tasks carefully on a
separate piece of paper. You
can then check whether your
answers are correct on page

The space shuttle will transport
you into space.

Space Center

Welcome to the Space Center and congratulations on being chosen to join the latest class of trainee astronauts. You are one of the lucky few. Thousands of people apply to be space shuttle astronauts each year, but only a handful are chosen. You were selected because you are fit, educated, and have the personal qualities necessary to be a good crew member. At the Space Center we are going to build on these qualities and help you develop the knowledge and skills you will need in space. The four key people who will guide and assist you through your four training modules will introduce themselves to you. Pay attention to what they have to say – the success of your mission may depend on it.

Good luck and, when the time comes, enjoy your space trip!

MODULE CONTENTS

Steve Harrison –
Space Coordinator

David Bridges –
Astronaut Trainer

Ellen Collins –
Scientific Advisor

Owen Mitchell –
Space Shuttle Pilot

MODULE A
In this module you will learn what space is like, how far you will be traveling into space, and find out about the vehicle you will travel in.

MODULE B
In this module you will be issued your gear, complete your practical training in the simulators, and practice the emergency procedures.

MODULE C
In this module you will be briefed about the launch and find out what it is really like to live and work in space.

MODULE D
In this module you will learn about space stations, how to dock with them in the space shuttle, and how to make a successful return home.

Destination Space
6

Vehicle for Space
8

The Orbiter Space Plane
10

Selecting Your Gear
12

Astronaut Training
14

Surviving in Space
16

Countdown and Blastoff
18

Everyday Life in Space
20

Working Outside
22

Working in Spacelab
24

Space Rendezvous
26

Back to Earth
28

Index
30

Destination Space

"Hello, I'm Steve Harrison, Space Coordinator, and I'm here to start you on your journey to space. We'll be working together for 'Module A' of your astronaut training."

To gain astronaut status you must travel at least 50 miles (80 km) above Earth. That is not far – it takes about eight minutes in the space shuttle. However, as you leave Earth and move through its atmosphere, the environment changes and becomes deadly to humans. In this training session we will compare Earth with space, discuss how the space shuttle is used, and look at its work with other spacecraft.

SPACE HIGHWAY

Every year about a hundred craft are launched into Earth's atmosphere and beyond. Some transport people, some collect and transmit information, some carry out experiments, and some observe the Solar System. How far they go above Earth depends on the type of job they are doing.

Life in space

You cannot survive in space without support and protection. In space there is no oxygen to breathe, the temperature is either hot enough to turn you into toast, or cold enough to freeze you solid, and the air pressure is so low that your body liquids evaporate. The pull of gravity is weaker than it is on Earth.

AIR	No air
TEMPERATURE	-150 to 250° F
RANGE	(-101 to 121° C)

Thermosphere – between 50 and 298 miles (80 and 480 km) high

The Russian space station, *Mir*, has been manned by astronauts since February 198 and is about 217 mile (350 km) above Eart

Satellites are about 155 621 miles (250 to 1,000 km high as they trav around Earth

Life on Earth

The conditions on Earth suit you perfectly. The air contains oxygen for breathing, the pressure of the air allows you to breathe easily, and your surroundings are neither too hot nor too cold. At Earth's surface the pull of gravity keeps your feet firmly on the ground, but you can still move around with ease.

AIR	78% nitrogen, 21% oxygen, 1% other gases
TEMPERATURE	-94 to 131° F
RANGE	(-70 to 55° C)

Mesosphere – between 31 and 50 miles (50 and 80 km) high

Earth's surface

Stratosphere – between 7 and 31 miles (11 and 50 km) high

Troposphere – up to 7 miles (11 km) high

Meteor shower

Helium-filled balloon

Glider

Jumbo jet

Mount Everest

Gravity to weightlessnes

The farther you travel above Earth, the farthe you move away from Earth's gravity. If a spacecra does not travel far enough to get away completel it will be held in an orbit around Earth. As th shuttle orbits, the surface curves away beneath i so it is constantly falling around the Earth. Th makes it and everything in it feel weightles

Earth's atmospher

Earth's atmosphere is made up of five main layers. Th troposphere is the nearest layer. Most of the weather occu here. Next comes the stratosphere, which is a calm region The mesosphere can be very cold, -148° F (-100° C). In th next layer, the thermosphere, the air is thin and very ho

Into space

There is no neat dividing line between the exosphere and space – one fades into the other. This is where you travel in the space shuttle.

YOU ARE HERE
The space shuttle flies between 124 and 621 miles (200 and 1,000 km) above Earth's surface.

Exosphere – between 298 and 621 miles (480 and 1,000 km) high

The *Hubble Space Telescope* travels around Earth at an average height of 311 miles (500 km).

PACE SHUTTLE IN ACTION

he space shuttle is capable of carrying out a number f tasks, from scientific experiments to launching other raft, and your mission could involve any one of them.

Sometimes the space shuttle carries a mobile laboratory called Spacelab. It consists of a laboratory and pallets full of experiments.

Often the space shuttle is used to release satellites into space. It can also be used to capture and repair them.

The *Hubble Space Telescope* was launched by the space shuttle. Later crews also repaired the telescope while in space.

Space probes investigate our Solar System. The space shuttle is used as a launch pad to send them into space.

The space shuttle can dock with space stations, like *Mir*, to deliver and collect astronauts and supplies. It can also be used to build space stations.

Planning an orbit

The route you take around Earth for your mission is determined well before your date of departure. But whatever distance you are from Earth, each day you travel from brilliant sunny skies to total darkness.

TASK 1

Based on the information given about the space shuttle and its orbit in the diagram, figure out how long it takes to complete one orbit of Earth.

TIP
Remember to convert your calculations into hours and minutes.

The space shuttle is traveling at an average speed of 16,486.5 mph (26,548.5 kph).

One orbit of Earth is about 24,750 miles (39,823 km).

TASK 2

Using your answer to Task 1, figure out how many times you see the Sun rise in 24 hours (one Earth day).

OBSERVATION
Before you fly into space, it may be possible for you to spot the space shuttle in orbit. Observe the early morning or early evening sky. The space shuttle looks like a moving star.

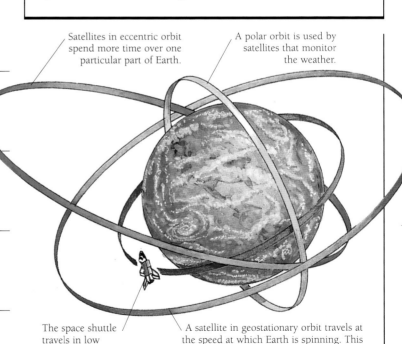

Satellites in eccentric orbit spend more time over one particular part of Earth.

A polar orbit is used by satellites that monitor the weather.

The space shuttle travels in low Earth orbit.

A satellite in geostationary orbit travels at the speed at which Earth is spinning. This means it stays over the same part of Earth during its complete orbit.

Orbiting Earth

Spacecraft orbit, or circle around, Earth. The orbit they take determines the distance and the speed at which they travel. There are four main orbital paths: polar orbit, low Earth orbit, eccentric orbit, and geostationary orbit. The space shuttle follows a path in low Earth orbit.

MODULE 🄰 ▢ ▢ ▢

Vehicles for Space

■ The space shuttle is the only successful reusable space vehicle in the world. Like other spacecraft, the space shuttle is boosted into space by its rockets. But unlike any other craft, it glides back to Earth to be used again by a new crew of astronauts. After the completion of a mission, the space shuttle can be reassembled for another launch in just six and a half days.

THE TOTAL SYSTEM

The space shuttle is made up of three parts: a reusable plane, called an orbiter, two solid fuel rockets, which are recovered and reused on later missions, and an expendable (throwaway) fuel tank.

The assembled vehicle is 184 ft (56 m) high and 78 ft (24 m) wide.

The fuel tank supplies the orbiter's main engines during blastoff and ascent.

The two solid fuel booster rockets propel the space shuttle away from Earth.

The orbiter is about the size of a small airplane.

The space shuttle is assembled in the vehicle assembly building – one of the largest buildings in the world.

FLIGHT PROFILE

The complete space shuttle system is together for only a few minutes at the start of your journey. Once the fuel tank is empty and the rockets have burned out, they both fall off, leaving you and the rest of the crew in the orbiter to complete your mission.

6. The orbiter's on-board engines are used to reach low Earth orbit.

7. Astronauts work inside and outside the orbiter as it travels around Earth.

8. The orbiter positions itself, ready to return to Earth.

The fuel tank falls back into Earth's atmosphere and breaks up over the ocean.

4. The two solid fuel rockets are discarded.

5. The fuel tank is released, leaving only the orbiter.

Launch to landing

Your trip in space will last four to seven days. As you travel, some ground crew people will retrieve the reusable parts of the space shuttle, while others will monitor your progress in space. Everyone will be on standby for your return.

9. The orbiter moves downward through Earth's atmosphere.

As the rockets fall back to Earth, their parachutes open.

3. The space shuttle blasts off and moves upward, away from the launch pad.

Waiting ships recover the two rockets from the ocean.

1. The space shuttle is made ready in the vehicle assembly building.

10. The orbiter gets ready for a high-speed glide onto the runway.

2. The space shuttle travels on the crawler transporter to the launch pad.

12. The orbiter glides in to land on the extra-long runway.

11. The orbiter's landing gear is lowered.

...ll of fuel

...e external fuel tank is the ...gest and heaviest part of the ...ace shuttle. At blastoff it ...rns 64,000 gallons (242,240 ...ers) of fuel a minute.

The fuel tank is 154 ft (47 m) long and 27.6 ft (8.4 m) in diameter.

Liquid oxygen tank

Liquid oxygen fuel pipe leading to orbiter

Liquid hydrogen tank

Liquid hydrogen fuel pipe leading to orbiter

The rocket ignites here.

On ignition the fuel burns from top to bottom in all four segments of each rocket.

Each rocket is 149.2 ft (45.5 m) long and 12.2 ft (3.7 m) in diameter.

The four central segments contain the solid fuel.

...ocket power

...e two solid fuel ...cket boosters ...ve to be powerful ...ough to lift the ...stem off the ...ound. When the ...el is lit, hot gases ...e forced down- ...ard through a ...zzle. This propels ...e space shuttle in ...e opposite direction.

...t gases escape from the ...cket, forcing the space ...ttle upward.

The parachutes are stored in the nose.

Small rockets are used to separate the rocket from the space shuttle.

The orbiter, rockets, and fuel tank are fixed together for blastoff.

Pipes deliver fuel from the fuel tank to the orbiter.

During liftoff and ascent the orbiter is powered by fuel from the external fuel tank.

Small rockets are fired to separate the rocket from the space shuttle.

Escaping gravity

The space shuttle's speed increases quickly as it moves away from Earth. It needs to go fast to get away from gravity's pull and achieve its low Earth orbit. The speed, or orbital velocity, needed for this is 4.9 mps (7.9 kps). The space shuttle's orbit is circular so its speed is constant. The speed of a spacecraft on an eccentric orbit varies. It moves fastest when closest to Earth.

b
a – low Earth orbit

b – eccentric orbit

c – start of distant orbit

TASK 1
Using the diagrams work out which is the space shuttle's orbit, **a** or **b**.

TASK 2
Would the orbital velocity of a spacecraft on path **b** be fastest or slowest when farthest away from Earth?

TASK 3
Is path **c** the start of a circular or an eccentric orbit?

The crawler moves at about 1 mph (1.6 kph).

The crawler transporter is 20 ft (6.1 m) high, 131 ft (40 m) long, and 114 ft (34.7 m) wide.

Ready for launch
The space shuttle is put together on the crawler transporter, the largest land vehicle in the world. Slowly the crawler transporter moves toward the launch pad.

Piggyback transport
The orbiter is not always launched from its last landing site. A specially adapted Boeing 747 aircraft can carry the orbiter on its back between different sites.

The Orbiter Space Plane

■ The space shuttle's orbiter is one of the most amazing vehicles ever built. About the size of a small airplane, it contains everything you and the rest of the crew will need to survive for the duration of your mission, and is fully equipped to carry out the necessary space work. In this training session we will look at the orbiter, how it is powered, and how to operate it.

ORBITER FLEET

You will travel in one of four orbiters: *Columbia*, *Discovery*, *Atlantis*, or *Endeavour*. They are all identical in size and structure.

LENGTH	122 ft (37 m)
HEIGHT	57 ft (17.4 m)
WINGSPAN	78 ft (24 m)

Top view

Side view

WEIGHT	187,000 lb (84,778 kg)
CARGO CAPACITY	50,000 lb (22,680 kg)

Bottom view

Payload bay

The large cargo area in the orbiter is called the payload bay. It is 60 ft (18.3 m) long by 15 ft (4.6 m) wide. Satellites, space probes, or Spacelab are carried up to space inside the payload bay.

PITCH
The orbiter moves up or down in a vertical circle.

ROLL
The orbiter turns upside down and back again from wing to wing.

YAW
The orbiter moves left to right in a horizontal circle.

Space moves

Unlike an airplane flying in Earth's atmosphere, in space the orbiter cannot rely on friction from air to slow it down. This means if you move the orbiter in one direction, you must move it in the opposite direction to slow down. The three moves the orbiter can make are yaw, roll, and pitch.

Remote manipulator arm

Pilot's and commander's seats

Rearview windows into payload bay

Payload bay

Payload bay controls

Flight deck

Double-wheeled nose landing gear

Space radiator (inside doo

Ladder to mid deck

Forward control thrusters

Entrance and exit hatch

Payload bay doors

Moving the orbiter

Once in space, you may need to move the orbiter to correct your orbital path, to make a space rendezvous, or to come out of orbit on your way home.

TASK 1

In each case, from **a** to **h**, figure out whether you need to roll, pitch, or yaw to go from the first to the second position.

a b c d e f g h

TIP
Some cases may require more than one type of movement.

Rudder splits into two halves.

Three main engines used during blastoff

There are two orbital maneuvering system engines

Thrusters help make small movements in space.

Thermal insulation tiles cover the orbiter.

Vertical tail

Camera records arm's movements and sends pictures to flight deck.

Handrails used during outside activity

The body flap helps control the orbiter during landing.

Elevon for use during landing

Engine power

The orbiter has two sets of engines: the main engines, which help propel the space shuttle into space during blastoff and ascent, and the orbital maneuvering system engines, which control the orbiter's speed and direction in space.

Main landing gear

The delta-shaped wing has no function in space, but helps the orbiter glide in to land.

Cooling down

You must open the payload bay doors as soon as you reach low Earth orbit. This allows the excess heat from the orbiter's system to escape through the radiators, and stops the orbiter from overheating.

USA

Selecting Your Gear

"My name is David Bridges. We'll be working together in 'Module B.' I'll help you prepare for everyday life in space and show you how to overcome the problems you may encounter."

■ In this training session we will look at the personal items you will use during your space flight. These include clothing, crew equipment, and sighting aids; they are either packed away in the orbiter, or given to you before takeoff. Pay attention, because each item has been carefully designed and what you wear and use depends on the type of job you are doing.

Packed up

All your personal items wi[ll] be packed in storage tray[s] before takeoff and secured in lockers in th[e] mid deck ready for use[.]

Also packed away will be special-issue underwear – the longer your flight, the more changes you will get!

CREW CLOTHES

There are three types of space outfits: a partial pressure suit for launch and return, in-flight garments for everyday orbiter life, and an extravehicular mobility unit (EMU) space suit to protect you[r] if you go outside the orbiter.

Partial pressure suit

This one-piece suit has an inflata[ble] bottom section that stops blood from pooling in the lower half of your body. This reduces the dang[er] of you fainting when the spacecra[ft] returns from weightlessness to Ea[rth] gravity. The suit also has a parach[ute] harness and pack, which you'll ne[ed] if an emergency arises and you have to leave the orbiter.

You will be helped into your suit by a technician before you enter the orbiter.

The badge on your left breast displays your name.

In-flight garments

After the ascent, you can change into your in-flight garments. These include pants, lined zip-up jackets, knit shirts, and sleeping shorts. They have to be made of materials that are both comfortable and flame-resistant.

Flapped pockets cover the outside of the pants and jackets and are used for storing items such as pens, a pocketknife, a flashlight, food sticks, sunglasses, and scissors.

All the clothes come in three different sizes: small, medium, and large.

The su[it's] bright co[lor] makes y[ou] easy to s[pot] for rescu[e]

Footwear

There is no need for shoes inside the orbiter. These slipper-socks with soft, thickened soles will keep your feet warm.

Getting dressed

The EMU space suit is kept in the airlock and this is where you will put it on. Getting into the space suit can be tricky, and will probably take about 15 minutes.

The urine collection device is emptied later in the orbiter.

Pull on the liquid-cooled underwear over the urine collection device.

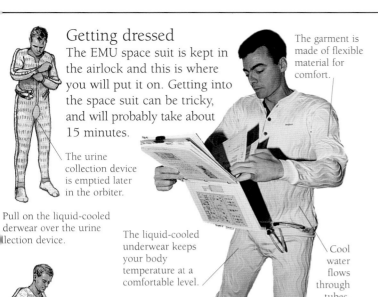

The garment is made of flexible material for comfort.

The liquid-cooled underwear keeps your body temperature at a comfortable level.

Cool water flows through tubes.

The space suit is in two pieces. First, pull on the pants with built-in shoes.

EMU SPACE SUIT

The EMU space suit, for working outside, provides oxygen for you to breathe and keeps the air pressure around your body at the right level. The suit also protects you from the extreme heat and cold of space, and from fast-moving space dust.

The helmet's visor provides protection against ultraviolet and infrared radiation from the Sun.

The primary life-support system, or PLSS, backpack contains oxygen for breathing.

The top half of the suit hangs on the airlock wall. Put it on by moving up into it.

The gloves are the only item of clothing made to your specific requirements.

The "Snoopy Cap" contains headphones and a microphone for two-way communication.

Bearings in the shoulder, arm, wrist, and waist joints allow you to move with ease.

Fit the two halves tightly together. Next, put on the communications cap, gloves, and finally the helmet.

Crew equipment

There are lots of useful items packed into storage lockers on the orbiter for everyone to use. There is also a selection of cameras for taking photographs and video films. Use them to record your trip.

On-board crew equipment:
- Flashlights
- Scissors
- Pocket food
- Plastic mirrors
- Pens and pencils
- Swiss army knives
- Sunglasses and pouches
- Emergency medical kit
- Personal hygiene kits
- Watches and watchbands

On-board sighting aids:
- Cameras
- Video cameras
- Binoculars
- Star and Earth maps

You can take a personal stereo and your favorite music CD if you wish.

Personal items

There may be something you want to take on your trip. Everything must be approved, but if it is small, light, and not a fire hazard, you will probably be allowed to take it.

TRAINING TASK 4

Taking photos in space

The success of your photographs depends on the amount of light reaching the film. You will not need as much light for close-up photographs as you will for long-distance photographs. You can control the amount of light entering the camera by altering the aperture (front opening), and the length of time it is open. The aperture is indicated by a series of "*f*" numbers – the smaller the number, the larger the aperture, and the shutter time can be set to be open for fractions of a second.

TASK 1

Which of the settings, **a** or **b**, would you use for: 1) a close-up of an astronaut eating inside the orbiter, and 2) a long-distance view of your hometown on Earth?

a) 5.6 and 1/60
b) 5.6 and 1/500

TIP
The *f* number range is: 1.4, 2, 2.8, 4, 5.6, 8, 11, 16, 22. The exposure times are: 1/60, 1/125, 1/250, 1/500, 1/1000 of a second.

Astronaut Training

■ During this training session you will learn about the mission simulators. These help you become familiar with the practical aspects of your journey without actually traveling to space. In the months before takeoff you will go through the details of your mission, from launch to landing, using computer software. You will practice these mission procedures over and over again until they become second nature.

MISSION SIMULATORS

Simulators are large pieces of training equipment that are built to re-create the conditions you will find in space. They include exact copies of sections of the orbiter.

Orbiter simulators
The two orbiter simulators each consist of the nose end of an orbiter and are positioned as if ready for launch. One of them is fixed, but the other moves to simulate takeoff.

Flight-deck controls
In the flight deck mock-up you can practice using the controls for all parts of the flight – prelaunch, ascent, orbit operations, reentry, and landing.

Working practice
You can practice payload bay procedures using these mock-ups of the payload bay and the flight deck. They help you become familiar with the remote manipulator system.

Inside t orbi simulator y lie in a fli chair rea for "takeof

Images of Ea from space or t landing runw are project onto t windows, so th you see exac what astona see during a r space tr

Displays a controls are t same as in t real orbit

Remo manipulator a

You can operate t manipulator arm move cargo and out of t payload b

The commander (left) and pilot (right) use the flight deck mock-up to practice landing on the runway.

A large drum-shaped helium balloon simulates a satellite cargo.

You can look through the flight deck windows into the payload bay and watch the manipulator arm move.

Life-size orbiter payload bay

Coming
down

Gravity and weight

You have weight because Earth's gravity pulls on you. An increase in gravity's pull makes you heavier, a decrease makes you lighter. As you move away from Earth toward space, gravity's pull is lessened and you become lighter.

TASK 1

Imagine you could stand at different heights above Earth. If you weighed 220.5 lb (100 kg) on Earth (at **a**), figure out your weight at positions **b**, **c**, and **d**.

TIP
To figure out your weight, divide your weight on Earth by the square of the radial distance from Earth's center. (The radial distance is the distance from the center of a sphere to any point on its surface.)

d Radial distance from Earth's center is 2.5.

c Radial distance from Earth's center is 2.

b Radial distance from Earth's center is 1.5.

a Radial distance from Earth's center is 1.

Earth

oing
p

will
erience
ghtless-
s like
about
imes
ne day.

aining for weightlessness

r all but the very start and end of your trip
u will feel weightless. To get used to this
u can travel in the KC-135 aircraft. The
atless airliner flies to a height of 6.5 miles
0.5 km), then quickly descends to 4.5
les (7.3 km). During this descent you will
weightless for about 20 seconds.

epeat practice

your particular mission
volves any extravehicular
tivity you will practice
rforming the tasks in an
MU suit until you feel
e you could do them in
ur sleep.

eightless-environment training facility

hen you are underwater the effect of gravity on your body
lessened, as it is in space, so this deep pool of water is
here you practice working in a weightless environment.
e submerged payload bay allows you to practice your
ecific EVA jobs. Wearing an EMU suit, you can attach
urself to the remote manipulator arm, then carry out
pairs using the tools you will work with in space.

Surviving in Space

In this training session we will look at some of the problems you may encounter in space. They could have to do with you and how your body reacts to space life, or they might be because of a malfunction with the shuttle or one of its systems. Whatever the nature of the problem, a solution procedure has been formed for it and ground control and the rest of the crew will be on hand to help.

EMERGENCIES NEAR EARTH

It is possible that a problem may occur in Earth's environment, either as you wait strapped in your seat on the launchpad, or during takeoff and landing.

Rapid exit

If you are traveling through Earth's atmosphere and cannot land, use the side hatch in the mid deck to exit the craft. First adjust the deck pressure so that it is the same as the pressure outside. Then put the escape pole through the side hatch, slide down the pole, and let go at the end.

The parachute in your partial pressure suit opens automatically.

The whole crew can bail out in less than 90 seconds in this way.

SPACE SICKNESS

Most astronauts feel sick during the first few days in space. In a weightless environment your internal organs and body fluids shift position because there is no gravity pulling them downward. This can cause nausea, headaches, sweating, and vomiting.

At the start of the trip your nose is blocked because your sinuses are congested with extra fluid.

Your face looks puffy as fluids move upward.

In space your heart does not need to pump as hard as it does on Earth and can get weak.

Your bones become weaker as minerals such as calcium are lost.

The weightlessness in space makes you "stand" on your toes with your knees bent, known as the "bird-legs" effect.

Your kidneys get rid of about 3.5 pints (2 liters) of fluid in the first few days.

In space you are 0.3-0.75 in (1-2 cm) taller than you are on Earth because the vertebrae in your spine float apart.

Steel baskets

In the 30 seconds before countdown ends and access to the launch tower is removed, you can escape from the orbiter in one of the seven steel baskets attached to the tower.

Armored vehic

If you need to abandon t orbiter before takeoff, armored vehicle will transp you away from the launchpa It can move across rou; terrain to take the shorte route to safe

The armored vehicle protects you from an explosion.

PACE EMERGENCIES

ghts on the control panels, and
arms that sound throughout the
biter and in your headset,
ll alert you if something
nusual happens during
ur space flight.

yload doors

he of the problems you may
ve is closing the payload doors.
he automatic closing system
ls, you will have to close the
ors manually. Put on your EMU
t and go outside to assess the
uation. Discuss the problem
th the crew and ground
ntrol before carrying
t the correction
ocedure.

orbiter cannot
rn to Earth
il the payload
rs are closed.

bandon ship

omething goes seriously wrong,
u may have to abandon the orbiter
d transfer to another craft. If this
ppens, put on either an EMU suit or
artial pressure suit. The EMU suit
an oxygen supply and provides
protection until you are
safe in the second craft.

Monitoring your body

You must stay fit in space and be aware of your state of
health. However, to know whether you are healthy or not,
you need to know what is normal. Answer the questions
below to assess what you know about the human body.

TASK 1

1. What is the normal temperature of a healthy human being?
a) 95° F (35° C)   b) 98.6° F (37° C)   c) 102.2° F (39° C)

2. Using what you have learned so far about space, what do
you think might happen to your blood if you pricked your
finger in the orbiter and it started to bleed?

3. Dust does not settle in space, but floats around inside the
orbiter, gets in your nose, and makes you sneeze. How many
times a day on average do you think you might sneeze in
space? a) 5   b) 50   c) 100

Escape ball

When abandoning the orbiter in space,
astronauts wearing partial pressure suits
should get into a personal rescue enclosure.
These 34-in (86-cm) inflatable balls are
pressurized and are just big enough for one
person to sit inside cross-legged. The EMU-
suited crew can then transfer the personal
rescue enclosures to the second craft.

The outer
material protects
the astronaut
against the
extreme
temperatures
of space.

The pressurized
atmosphere inside the
ball protects the
astronaut against the lack
of pressure in the
environment outside.

All crew members
wear a headset under
their helmet to
communicate with
the rest of the crew.

EMU-suited
astronauts have
enough oxygen to
last seven and a
half hours.

The oxygen
in the escape
ball lasts for
three hours.

Oxygen is fed
from a separate
unit into the
face mask.

Handle or
attachment ring
for moving the ball

Countdown and Blastoff

"Hello, I'm Ellen Collins, your Scientific Advisor and instructor for 'Module C.' I've flown on two space shuttle missions and can tell you what it is like to live, work, and travel in space."

■ In this training session, we will take a look at your launch into space. It is really a short part of your whole trip, but in the few minutes it takes, you will have lots of new experiences. Although you will have practiced the launch hundreds of times in the orbiter simulator, this is never as exhilarating as the rush of noise, the vibrations, and the surge of motion that you encounter on your first real trip into space.

COUNTDOWN TO LAUNCH

TIME PRIOR TO TAKEOFF (T)	PROCEDURE	ACTION
hrs mins secs **5.00.00**	Begin launch day	Wake, breakfast, and dress. Meanwhile, fuel is pumped into the external fuel tank.
1.50.00	Enter the orbiter	Enter the orbiter and climb into your seats. Secure your safety straps.
1.30.00	Check communications with launch control	Launch control contacts you on air-to-ground intercom and air-to-air channels.
1.25.00	Check communications with mission control	Mission control contacts you on air-to-ground channels.
1.10.00	Close the entrance and exit hatch	Ground crew closes and secures the side hatch.
0.20.00	Load the space shuttle computer	Load the final mission data into the computer.
0.09.00	Go for automatic countdown	Reposition timer switch to "start." Automatic countdown begins.
0.00.30	Cut electrical links with Earth	Switch management of launch from launch control to onboard computers.

UP AND AWAY

Your launch into space is automatically controlled by onboard computers, but this does not mean that you have nothing to do. Your main job is to check everythin runs smoothly and to solve any problems that may aris

You hear the orbital maneuvering system engines ignite and the orbiter moves into low Earth orbit.

You feel weightless and you can look out the window and see Earth.

T +50 minutes
You are in low Earth orbit, about 250 miles (400 km) above Earth.

T +10 minutes 39 seconds
Your speed is 17,500 mph (28,157.5 kph) and your height is 170 miles (273.5 km).

ission control

hen you reach orbit, launch control passes you er to mission control, a team of people on rth that monitors your every movement. u will be in constant contact with ssion control for the rest of your flight.

Although you cannot see it, the empty fuel tank is ejected from the orbiter.

T +8 minutes 54 seconds
Your speed is 17,000 mph (27,353 kph) and your height is 73 miles (117.5 km).

View from space

There are two sure signs you have reached space. First, if you loosen your straps you will start to float across the orbiter. If you can control yourself, head for a window. There you will find the second sign. The view is breathtaking and one you will never forget.

-2 minutes 7 seconds r speed is 3,098 mph 972 kph) and your height 32 miles (51 km).

You see a bright flash of light as the empty rockets are fired off.

hin thirty seconds move out of th's blue sky blackness.

e orbiter ates wildly ou lift off launch

T +11 seconds
Your speed is 76 mph (123 kph).

Takeoff!

As the space shuttle accelerates you are pushed back into your seat. The force is three times the strength of gravity, which means you suddenly feel three times as heavy as you do on Earth.

TRAINING TASK

⑦

Space noise

Your takeoff will probably be the noisiest time of your life. A space shuttle launch is one hundred million times louder than a normal conversation. The loudness of sounds is measured in decibels. Each ten decibel increase means the sound is ten times louder.

TASK 1

Use the graph to figure out how much louder a space shuttle launch is than: a) normal traffic and b) classroom noise.

TASK 2

Space is silent because there is no air in which sound can travel. But inside the orbiter, air is pumped around the cabins and life is pretty loud. Where do you think the noise inside the orbiter should go on the graph, position D, G, or I?

TIP
If a sound is 20 decibels (dB) louder it is 10 x 10 times louder.

KEY
A – No sound
B – Falling leaves
C – Normal conversation
D – ?
E – Busy office
F – Classroom noise
G – ?
H – Normal traffic
I – ?
J – Rock group
K – Space shuttle launch
L – Noise painful to ears
M – Large rocket launch

Everyday Life in Space

■ Almost everything you do during a normal day on Earth, such as eating, drinking, sleeping, going to the bathroom, and washing, you can do in space. You usually do these things automatically, but in the weightlessness of space you need to really think about your actions and the consequences of them. In this training session we will look at how best to perform everyday activities in space.

DOUBLE DECKER

Most of your time in space is spent inside the orbiter in the flight and mid decks. Together the decks contain everything you need to live and work during your mission. The decks actually feel larger than they look. In space you use the whole room, from floor to ceiling, not just the floor area as you do in rooms on Earth.

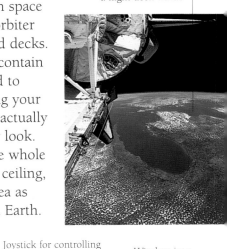

Your view of Earth from a flight deck window

Ship shape

In the weightless environment of space, everything floats around with the slightest push. Items that are set loose become a potential hazard. This is why it is more important now than at any other time in your life to clean up as you go along!

The storage lockers contain enough food to last the whole mission.

The flight and mid decks are situated in the orbiter's nose.

Controls used to contact mission control

Flight deck window

Joystick for controlling the remote manipulator arm

Window into payload bay

Controls for carrying out operations in the payload bay

Pilot's seat

Pilot's window

Bunk beds

Footholds secure your feet to the ground and stop you from floating around

Flight deck

Toilet

Everything in the flight and mid decks is stored in lockers, or fastened onto the walls with Velcro.

Mid deck

Running machine for personal exercise

Door to airlock

Airlock with exit to the payload bay

Ladder allows access from flight to mid deck

A DAY IN THE ORBITER

Secure the food and cutlery tray to your leg.

Dried fruit and nuts are ready to eat.

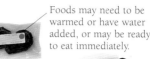
Foods may need to be warmed or have water added, or may be ready to eat immediately.

Foods are in individual packages.

Drinks are usually taken from resealable containers, but you may have to test a can adapted for use in space.

7:00 hrs Brushing up
Using the toilet is easy – just fasten yourself in before you start! Use wet wipes to wash your face and hands. If a crew member needs to shave, he must make sure he vacuums up before the hairs start floating around.

07:30 hrs Flying food
You can use fingers, knives, forks, spoons, and chopsticks to eat. The main difficulty is trying to get the food from the tray into your mouth. Eating from one package at a time will help you avoid losing control of your food.

Small, light personal items, such as a flute, can be taken on your flight.

Your bunks have sheets with restraints to stop you from floating off.

Footholds stop you from drifting around.

0:00 hrs Running time
Weightlessness makes it easy to move around, so your heart and muscles do not work very hard. Two hours a day on the running machine keeps you fit.

19:00 hrs Leisure time
At the end of the day you will have some free time and it is up to you how you use it. You may want to take photos from the window, or you can just sit and stare if you wish.

23:00 hrs Bedtime
As you settle down in one of the enclosed bunk beds, another crew member gets up and starts the next day's activities.

TRAINING TASK

8

TASK 1

In space, astronauts take turns to prepare meals. Using the tables at right, prepare five different meals for yourself and four others for a day. Try to satisfy the following needs:

Astronaut 1 – that's you and you know what you like
Astronaut 2 – does not eat meat or fish
Astronaut 3 – no special requirements
Astronaut 4 – does not eat eggs or nuts
Astronaut 5 – never feels hungry

For breakfast, each astronaut can have two foods each, and for lunch and dinner two from list A and one from list B for each meal. The astronauts should also have one drink for each meal, and up to two extra if needed. During the whole day each astronaut is allowed two snacks if desired. Finally, the daily intake for each astronaut must add up to between 2,500 and 3,000 calories.

TIP
Take care to note how many packs of a food you are using – don't run out!

Foods	Packs	Calories
BREAKFAST		
Cornflakes	2	200
Muesli	2	200
Bran Flakes	1	200
Bread roll and jam	4	240
Scrambled eggs	3	300
Dried fruit	3	150
SNACKS		
Peanuts	3	150
Shortbread	2	150
Dried fruit	3	150
Chocolate bar	2	150
DRINKS		
Apple	5	100
Orange	5	100
Chocolate	4	140
Strawberry	4	170
Coffee	5	20
Tea	5	20

Foods	Packs	Calories
LUNCH AND DINNER		
LIST A		
Turkey and potatoes	2	250
Meatballs	2	350
Chicken and rice	2	350
Tunafish and rice	1	350
Salmon and vegetables	2	350
Scrambled egg	1	300
Tomato soup and roll	2	300
Salmon and bread	2	350
Cheese and bread	3	350
Peanut butter and bread	1	350
Broccoli au gratin	3	250
Cauliflower cheese	3	250
Potatoes au gratin	5	250
Rice	5	300
LIST B		
Chocolate pudding	3	150
Strawberry gelatin	4	150
Peach rice pudding	4	150
Lemon pudding	2	370

Working Outside

■ One of the highlights of your trip will be carrying out extravehicular activity, or EVA. This means you work outside the orbiter. Your work outside will involve either capturing, repairing, and launching a satellite, launching a space probe, or testing new equipment in the weightless environment of space. In this training session you will learn how to perform these tasks.

Handy machinery

During a mission you may use the remote manipulator system, or RMS. The RMS is made up of a robotic arm and its control system, which is in the flight deck. The RMS provides a platform on which you can stand to test new equipment or carry out repairs.

The life-support backpack contains two tanks of air – all you need for your EVA.

You can speak or signal to crew members watching you as they control the RMS from the flight deck.

You use specially designed tools to carry out the repairs.

This astronaut is repairing the *Hubble Space Telescope.*

Safety straps hold your feet securely to the remote manipulator arm.

The telescope is held in place by the remote manipulator arm.

A satellite is launched from the space shuttle and set on its orbit in space.

Here the *Galileo* space probe is being released from *Atlantis's* payload bay.

Riding high

Satellites and space probes are launched from the payload bay into their orbits. This task is performed using the payload assistant module, PAM.

The satellite or space probe engine ignites.

The satellite or space probe is set on its orbital path.

4. The orbiter begins to correct its position.

1. A satellite or space probe is carried into space in the payload bay.

2. The orbiter maneuvers nose-down into PAM's launch position.

3. The satellite or space probe is ejected from the payload bay.

5. The orbiter continues along its orbital path.

PAM in actio

A satellite or space probe si in the payload bay inside specially designed cradle. T start the launch process, th cradle opens and a table, t which the satellite is attached starts to rotate. When the table going fast enough, springs eje the satellite. It moves off th table at about 3 fps (1 mps

CAPTURING A SATELLITE

This is the procedure you will follow to capture an orbiting satellite and return it to the payload bay for repair.

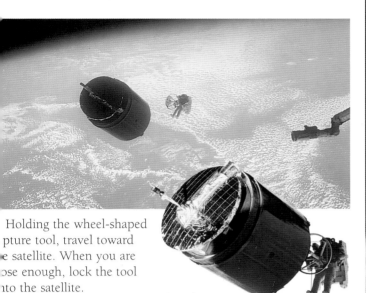

Holding the wheel-shaped capture tool, travel toward the satellite. When you are close enough, lock the tool into the satellite.

Once the captured satellite stops spinning you can head back to the orbiter.

2. Propel the satellite toward the orbiter. Another member of the crew will be waiting on the RMS. When you are close enough, attach the special fixture on the satellite onto the RMS arm.

A third member of the crew in the flight deck will control the RMS to pull you and the satellite into the payload bay. Secure the satellite to a fitting inside the payload bay.

Once the satellite is secure it can either be repaired in the payload bay or taken back to Earth for refitting and launch on a future mission.

Pack power
The manned maneuvering unit, or MMU, a backpack with rocket power, allows you to move around in space within about 328 ft (100 m) of the orbiter. You can steer the unit by using the hand controls at the end of each arm.

TRAINING TASK 9

Extravehicular activity
When you carry out an EVA task you will wear your EMU spacesuit. It provides all the oxygen necessary to keep you alive. The PLSS backpack contains enough oxygen for seven hours plus an extra safety supply of thirty minutes.

TASK 1
While repairing a satellite, you find that it is taking longer than expected. You have already used up half your oxygen and because you are rushing you are using the remainder at a faster rate.

Each half hour's worth of remaining oxygen is now being used up in twenty minutes. You still have two and a half hours of work ahead. Can you complete it without using your safety supply?

Working in Spacelab

■ You are going to space to work. In this training session we will look at the work carried out in Spacelab. A scientific laboratory that can fit into the orbiter's payload bay, Spacelab is owned by the European Space Agency and used by the international community. The research you do may be on behalf of a space agency, a university research department, or a commercial group.

THE SPACE LABORATORY

Spacelab is put together on Earth and taken into space on a mission dedicated to scientific experiments. It is made up of either a long or short cabin, and a varying number of pallets, depending on the nature and number of experiments. This illustration shows the short cabin with two pallets.

Spacelab sits in the payload bay.

Active flying

This is how Spacelab looked on its first flight in *Columbia*'s payload bay in 1983. About half of the experiments on board needed an astronaut's input. This meant working in the laboratory in addition operating the controls for instruments outside on the pallets.

Stargazing

Astronomer-astronauts can work with telescopes set on pallets in the payload bay. A telescope looking at the Sun will be used once every orbit. You will need to point the telescope at the correct part of the Sun and then instruct it to record what it sees.

Instrument for investigating Earth's magnetic field

Instrument for investigating the space environment

Telescope

Electron accelerator

Barium canisters

Solar panels

Windows in airlock give views of space.

Handrails for working outside

Experiments sit in racks on the walls.

Airlock

Airlock to move outside into space

Access tunnel from orbiter to Spacelab

Pallets are used to support instruments exposed to the space environment

The two pallets are linked together.

Single pallet

Cabin is pressurized and air is kept fresh.

Short cabin

Footholds in the floor

Insulation blanket helps keep Spacelab's temperature suitable for work in shirtsleeves

Pallet system

Each pallet is 10 ft (3 m) long and offers about 56 ft² (17 m²) for mounting experiments. Each has its own electrical power and cooling system.

EXPERIMENTING IN SPACE

The racks on the walls of Spacelab hold many different experiments. You may find yourself making crystals to help medical research, working with a flame to find out how fire spreads in space, or even watching shrimp eggs hatch.

Astronauts work in shifts in Spacelab.

Footholds in the floor help give a sense of "up" and "down."

The lack of gravity in space causes white roots to grow above, rather than below, the soil.

These mung-bean seedlings were grown in space from seeds.

Space life
Life-science experiments look at how space affects living things. Growing plants and observing small creatures, such as frogs and jellyfish, are common areas of experimentation.

Light work
Because you are weightless you cannot weigh yourself in space. However, you can measure your mass (the amount of material of which you are made) using the odd-looking body-mass measurement device. You can compare this with your mass on Earth as recorded before the mission.

Human experiments
Scientists are continually monitoring the effects of space flight on the human body. This means you may become the subject of an experiment.

You may have to wire yourself up to a machine and record the results in Spacelab.

Glove box
If you are carrying out an experiment that is dangerous to crew members, or might interfere with other work, you can use the "glove box." This is a small, sealed unit with a see-through front that fits into the wall racks. You use it by inserting your hands into gloves in the lower wall of the unit.

TRAINING TASK

10

Growing plants
Future astronauts may grow their own food and breathe oxygen produced by plants. On Earth, a seed has everything it needs to make it grow strong and healthy. It has water to help it form roots and shoots, light to make its leaves green, and gravity to ensure its roots grow downward to pick up lots of nutrients from the soil. In space, these things are not readily available.

KEY

Seed	🫘
Water	💧
Light	☀️
Gravity	⬇️

CONDITION CHART

A	🫘	💧	☀️	⬇️
B	🫘	💧	☀️	
C	🫘	💧		
D	🫘		☀️	
E	🫘	💧		⬇️

TASK 1
A seed on Earth is shown as A in the chart. Study B, C, D, and E, and figure out which seed has the best chance of developing roots, shoots, and green leaves.

TASK 2
In space, water can be fed to the seed through tubes, and lamps can be used to supply the necessary light. Which condition, B, C, D, or E, do you think is possible in space?

Space Rendezvous

"Hello, I'm Owen Mitchell, a space shuttle pilot. I've docked the orbiter with the Russian space station, and flown it home twice. In 'Module D' we'll look at space stations and your return journey."

■ The space shuttle orbiter is able to link up, or dock, with a space station, so in the future you may be picked for this type of mission. At present the orbiter travels to *Mir*, the Russian space station, but in a few years time this will be replaced by the bigger International Space Station. Shuttle astronauts on future trips will live and work aboard the station for weeks or months at a time.

SPACE STATIONS

Space stations are permanent orbiting spacecraft in whic astronauts can carry out long-term research in a space environment. Space stations also provide humans with a space home, and the work carried out in this unique setting may one day allow astronauts to have self-sufficient lives in space.

The orbiter usually stays docked to *Mir* for three to four days.

One Russian astronaut lived in *Mir* for a record 437 days.

Mir orbits Earth once every 92 minutes.

Mir space station
There are usually two or three Russians on board *Mir*, but it can house up to six crew members. Visiting astronauts arrive either by the Russian *Soyuz* craft or the orbiter

Sahara Desert
The red sand dunes in the center of the view are one of the most prominent features of the Sahara when seen from space.

The US at night
The bright spots in this photo are major cities in three American states: Indiana, Kentucky, and Ohio.

Great Lakes
The Great Lakes are visible from space. Lake Ontario is in the foreground.

SPACE VIEWS

One of the most fascinating things about being in space is looking out a window at Earth. It is lots of fun, but what you see can also be of use on Earth. Astronauts have helped track the path of a hurricane, and spotted ash plumes from volcanoes. Astronauts who stay on *Mir* have a tradition of taking a photograph of their home from space. It is a thrill to look down on your hometown from such a distance.

Detailed maps help you locate sites as you pass over them.

An artist's impression of the space shuttle docking with the International Space Station.

Viewing Earth

When you are in orbit in a space station, you will see some stunning views of Earth. At any one time you can see about 1,000 miles (1,609 km) of the curving Earth stretching from horizon to horizon.

TASK 1

Answer the following questions using the map to the right:
a) How many minutes will it take you to travel from A to B?
b) If Perth is on your western horizon and you look east, can you see Melbourne, yes or no?

TIP
The space station will travel over the Earth's surface at 290 mpm (466 kpm).

BUILDING A SPACE STATION

The orbiter is to play a big part in the construction and use of the International Space Station. As parts are ready, they will be transported by the orbiter and other craft, and attached together in space. This will take 70 flights over a five-year period.

International Space Station statistics:

LENGTH	290 ft (88 m)
WIDTH	356 ft (108.5 m)
WEIGHT	470 tons (426 tonnes)
CREW SIZE	Up to 7

When docking, two sets of hatches – one in the orbiter docking port and one in the station – are opened.

Two astronauts welcome orbiter crew members on board *Mir*.

Stairs are not needed – astronauts simply float between levels.

Space home
The living and working modules in the International Space Station will be pressurized and have a constant supply of fresh air. Equipment will be fitted along the walls and the floors will have footholds.

The service module provides life-support, thrusters, and habitation (toilet and hygiene) facilities.

Remote manipulator system for working outside the space station

Modules for living and working in

Laboratory

Rotating solar panels convert the Sun's energy into electricity for powering the station.

Radiators expel excessive heat.

Experiments and instruments exposed to space

Pressurized experiments module

Shuttle flights
When the International Space Station is completed, the orbiter will ferry crew, fresh food, water, and supplies to it. It will also bring returning crews and waste back to Earth.

Back to Earth

The return journey is the trickiest part of your trip. Not only must you make a careful reentry into Earth's atmosphere, but your landing must be perfect. Unlike an airplane, which can use its engines to take off again if it makes a mistake, when landing in the gliding orbiter, there is no second chance. So take your seat, strap yourself in, and get ready to learn about your return journey to Earth.

Touchdown -60 minutes
Your height is 175 miles (282 km) and your speed is 16,455 mph (26,482 kph) when you start the deorbit burn.

The orbital maneuvering system engines fire to slow down the orbiter.

The thrusters are used to turn the orbiter.

PREPARING TO LAND

About an hour and a half before touchdown you should drink a saline solution. This is a precaution against fainting, which can be brought on by dehydration during your descent. You then put on your partial pressure suit and strap yourself into your seat.

Pilot power
The commander (left) and the pilot (right) sit at the flight deck for the return journey. Apart from a brief communications blackout they are in contact with ground staff for all of the return flight.

Protective shell
There are about 32,000 tiles covering the outer surface of the orbiter. They stop the orbiter from burning up as it reenters Earth's atmosphere.

Once the orbiter has slowed down to about 69 mph (111 kph) the drag chute is ejected.

The rudder splits, keeping the orbiter stable as it slows down.

Silicon city
There are three types of tiles: white, gray, and black, each offering a different level of protection. Over 20,000 of the tiles are black and made from silica, like this one. The coating protects the orbiter from temperatures of up to 2,300° F (1,260° C).

The drag chute is 40 ft (12 m) in diameter.

Stopping the orbiter
The orbiter has special carbon breaks, a rudder that splits in two, and movable trailing edges, called elevons, on the wings to help it slow down. You will use a drag chute once you are on the runway to reduce the speed of the orbiter.

Touchdown -14 seconds
Just 1,099 ft (335 m) from the runway, you lower the landing gear and pull the orbiter's nose up to a 1.5° slope.

The movable trailing edges of the wings act as speed brakes.

Touchdown
You touch down on the 15,000-ft- (4,572-m-) long runway doing 215 mph (346 kph).

Touchdown -30 minutes
Your height is 76 miles (122 km) and your speed is 16,083 mph (25,877.5 kph) as you reenter Earth's atmosphere.

Communication breakdown

When you reenter Earth's atmosphere you will experience a communications blackout as the radio links with Earth are severed. This happens between approximately 53 miles (85 km) and 33 miles (53 km) above Earth. As you return to Earth, three main things are changing: your speed, height, and direction.

HEIGHT

- Deorbit burn
- Orbiter enters Earth's atmosphere
- Communications blackout begins
- Communications blackout ends
- Touchdown

62 miles (100 km)
50 miles (80 km)
37 miles (60 km)
25 miles (40 km)

FLIGHT PROFILE

TASK 1

If the orbiter is losing height at a rate of 1.25 miles (2 km) per minute, how long does the blackout last?

urning up
he angle of re-
try into Earth's
mosphere must be
refully calculated. If it is too steep,
ction caused by air makes the
biter burn up. If it is too shallow,
e orbiter skips out of the atmosphere.

Touchdown -20 minutes
When your height is 43.5 miles (70 km) the outside of the orbiter heats up to 2,500 °F (1,371 °C).

Touchdown -86 seconds
The final landing stage begins when you are 7.5 miles (12 km) from the runway and your speed is 424 mph (682 kph).

pace plane to glider
soon as the orbiter enters Earth's
mosphere air currents flow over
e craft. The delta wings that
ere redundant in space
ow help the craft
de as it descends.

Touchdown -32 seconds
When you are just 2 miles (3.2 km) from the runway and your speed is 351 mph (565 kph), you start to descend at a 20° slope.

Coming in to land

During the approach and landing stage, you drop at the rate of 1.9 miles (3 km) per minute. This is 20 times greater than the speed of an airliner's descent.

Touchdown -17 seconds
You are 3,540 ft (1,079 m) from the runway and traveling at a speed of 308 mph (496 kph).

MAXIMUM CAPACITY 4 PERSONS OR 1000 LBS.

Feet on the ground

Although you can unfasten your straps once the orbiter is on the ground, you have to wait for an hour before you can get out. The orbiter must cool down and be cleared of explosive or toxic (poisonous) fumes before you leave the craft.

NASA

United States

The body flap between the wings and below the main engines is used to position the orbiter during flight in Earth's atmosphere.

Index

A
air currents 29
airlock 20, 24
air pressure 6, 26
angle of reentry 29
armored vehicle 16
ascent 14
astronaut training 14-15
Atlantis 10, 22
atmosphere 6

B
barium canisters 24
blastoff 9, 18-19
body-mass measurement device 25
breathing 6
burning up 29

C
camera 11, 13
capturing a satellite 23
clothing 12-13
Columbia 10, 24
commander 28
communications blackout 28, 29
computer software 14
countdown procedure 18
crawler transporter 8, 9
crew equipment 12, 13

D
decks 20
delta-shaped wing 11
Discovery 10
docking with space stations 26-27
drag chute 28

E
Earth 6
eating in space 21
electron accelerator 24
elevons 11, 28
Endeavour 10
emergencies 17
engines 11
escape pole 16
escape procedures 16-17
European Space Agency 24
expendable fuel tank 8
exercising in space 21
exosphere 7
experimenting in space 7, 25
experiment pallets 24
external fuel tank 8, 9
extravehicular activity (EVA) 15, 22-23
extravehicular mobility unit (EMU)
    spacesuit 12, 13, 15, 17, 23

F
flight deck 10, 20
flight deck mock-up 14
flight profile 8
forward control thrusters 10
food 21

footholders 20
footwear 12
fuel tank 8

G
Galileo space probe 22
gravity 6, 9, 15
glove box 25
growing plants in space 25

H
handrails 11
Hubble Space Telescope 7, 8, 9, 22

I
ignition 9
in-flight garments 12
insulation blanket 24
International Space Station 26-27

K
KC-135 aircraft 15
kit 12

L
landing 14, 28-29
landing gear 8, 28
launch control 18, 19
launch pad 8
launching satellites 22
launching space probes 22
life-support backpack 22
living in space 20-21

M
malfunctions 16
manned maneuvering unit (MMU) 23
medical research 25
mesosphere 6
mid deck 20
Mir 6, 7, 26
mission control 18, 19
mission simulators 14-15

O
orbit operations 14
orbital maneuvering system 11, 19
orbits 7, 9
orbiter 8, 10-11
orbiter simulator 14

P
pallets 24
parachutes 9, 12, 16
partial pressure suit 12, 16, 17
payload assistant module (PAM) 22
payload bay 10, 17
payload bay mock-up 14
personal rescue enclosure 17
photography in space 13
piggyback transport 9
pitch 10
polar orbit 7

prelaunch 14
pressurized atmosphere 17
primary life-support system (PLSS) 13, 23

R
reentry 14
remote manipulator system (RMS) 10, 14, 15, 22
returning to Earth 28-29
rockets 8
roll 10
rudder 11, 28
runway 8

S
saline solution 28
satellites 6, 7, 22, 23
service module 27
sickness 16
sighting aids 12, 13
sleeping in space 21
slipper socks 12
"Snoopy" cap 13
solar panels 24, 27
solid fuel rocket boosters 8, 9
Soyuz 26
space dust 13
Spacelab 7, 10, 24-25
space probes 7, 10, 22
space radiators 11
space rendezvous 11
space stations 26-27
stratosphere 6
steel baskets 16
storage lockers 20
surviving in space 16-17

T
takeoff 18-19
telescope 22, 24
thermal protection tiles 11, 28
thermosphere 6
thrusters 11
toilet 20, 21
touchdown 28-29
transporting the space shuttle 9
troposphere 6

U
underwear, liquid-cooled 13
urine collection device 13

V
vehicle assembly building 8
vertical tail 11
viewing Earth from space 19, 26, 27

W
washing in space 21
weightlessness 6, 15, 16, 20
weightless-environment training facility 15

Y
yaw 10

Picture credits
Every effort has been made to trace the copyright holders. DK apologizes for any unintentional omissions and would be pleased, in such cases, to add an acknowledgment in future editions. The publisher would like to thank the following individuals, companies, and picture libraries for their kind permission to reproduce their photographs:
Genesis Space Photo Library/NASA: 2, 9cr, 12t, 12br, 13b, 16cr, 18cl, 21tl, 21tc, 21cl, 21c, 26b, 27tl; © NASA: 4b, 9c, 9br, 12bl, 13tl, 13tr, 13c, 14t, 14cl, 14c, 14bl, 14br, 15t, 15tl-tr, 15c, 15bl, 16cl, 16b, 17t, 17b, 19t, 19c, 20t, 21tcl, 21cr, 22cl, 22c, 22cr, 23tbl, 23c, 23b, 24t, 24cr, 25tl, 25tr, 25c, 25cbl, 25cbr, 26t, 26cl, 26c, 26cr, 27c, 27b, 28cl, 28cr, 28b, 29c, 29crb, 29b; **Popperfoto/Reuter:** 12c; Science Photo Library/NASA: 15br, 16t, 23tr, 23cl, 27cr; **Science & Society Picture Library/NASA:** 30. The Telegraph Colour Library: 17c, 23tl. **Jacket:** NASA: front bl, cr; **Science Museum:** front cl.

TRAINING TASK ANSWERS

Training Task 1
Task 1 – 1 hr 30 mins or 90 mins
Task 2 – 16 times

Training Task 2
Task 1 – a
Task 2 – slowest
Task 3 – eccentric

Training Task 3
Task 1
a Yaw, **b** Roll, **c** Pitch, **d** Pitch
e Pitch, **f** Roll, **g** Roll and pitch
h Pitch

Training Task 4
Task 1
1) **b**, 2) **a**

Training Task 5
Task 1
b – 98 lb (44 kg)
c – 55 lb (25 kg)
d – 35 lb (16 kg)

Training Task 6
Task 1
1) **b**
2) The blood would form a sphere and start to float round the orbiter.
3) **c**

Training Task 7
Task 1
a) 10,000 times louder
b) 100,000 times louder
Task 2 – G

Training Task 8
Task 1
Check your own answer. All menus, including that for astronaut 5, must add up to between 2,500 and 3,000 calories. Add up the number of times you have used each food and make sure it does not exceed the number of packs listed.

Training Task 9
Task 1 – No

Training Task 10
Task 1 – B
Task 2 – B. Everything except gravity can be provided in space.

Training Task 11
Task 1
a) 3 minutes
b) Yes

Training Task 12
Task 1 – 16 minutes

The module instructors featured in this book are fictitious and any resemblance to actual persons, living or dead, is purely coincidental.

Acknowledgments
DK would like to thank the following people for contributing to the production of this book: Stephen Bull for the training task illustrations, David Hughes and Jane Earland for consultancy, and Lia Foa.